th_
inspired
gardener

what makes us tick?

the inspired gardener

what makes us tick?

THE EDITORS OF ST. LYNN'S PRESS

st. lynn's
press

PITTSBURGH

The Inspired Gardener
what makes us tick?

by the Editors of St. Lynn's Press

ISBN-13: 978-0-9819615-3-8

Library of Congress Control Number: 2010937025
CIP information available upon request

First Edition, 2011

St. Lynn's Press · POB 18680 · Pittsburgh, PA 15236
412.466.0790 · www.stlynnspress.com

Book and Cover Design – Heidi Spurgin, Pure Design

Printed in the United States of America
on recycled paper using soy-based inks.

This title and all of St. Lynn's Press books may be purchased for educational,
business, or sales promotional use. For information please write:
Special Markets Department · St. Lynn's Press · POB 18680 · Pittsburgh, PA 15236

10 9 8 7 6 5 4 3 2 1

Welcome!

We wish you many happy moments
as you browse the pages of *The Inspired Gardener*.

The Editors

NONE CAN HAVE

A HEALTHY LOVE

FOR FLOWERS

UNLESS HE LOVES

THE WILD ONES.

FORBES WATSON

Except during

the nine months

before he draws

his first breath,

no man manages

his affairs as well

as a tree does.

GEORGE BERNARD SHAW

A
garden
is
never
so
good
as
it
will
be
next
year.

THOMAS COOPER

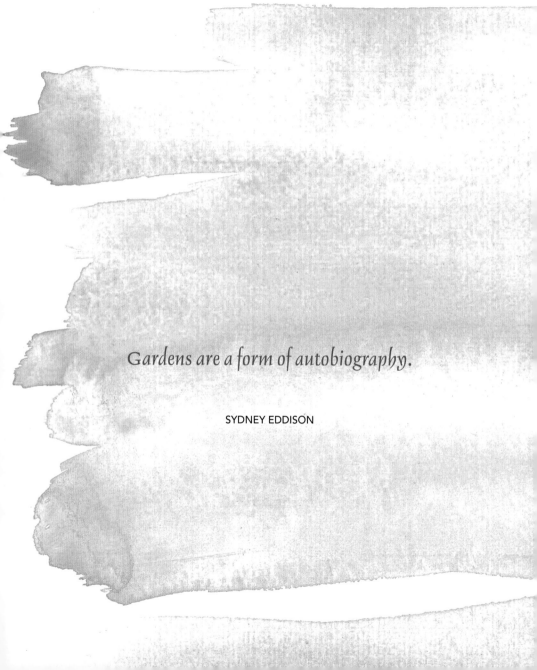

Gardens are a form of autobiography.

SYDNEY EDDISON

'IT IS AT THE EDGE OF A PETAL THAT LOVE WAITS.

WILLIAM CARLOS WILLIAMS

In the spring, at the end of the day, you should smell like dirt.

MARGARET ATWOOD

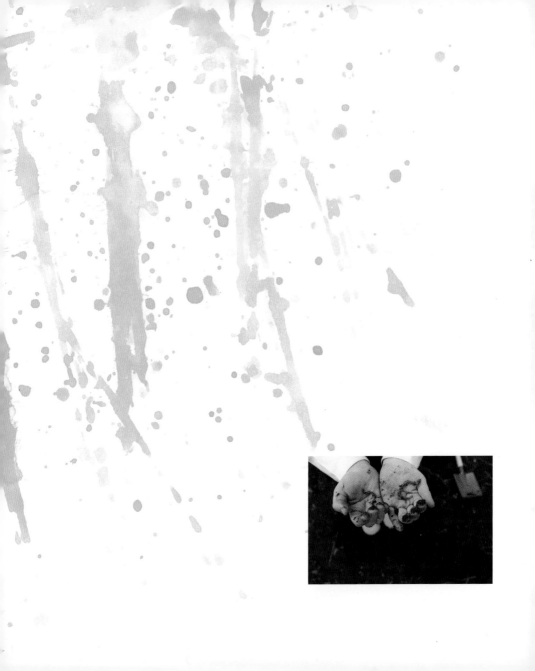

Why try to explain miracles to your kids
when you can just have them plant a garden?

ROBERT BRAULT

To see a thing in the seed, that is genius.

LAO TZU

Sometimes it seems

like the only time

I stop thinking

about growing organic food

is when I'm cooking

or eating it!

BARBARA PLEASANT

Like a great poet, Nature knows how to produce
the greatest effects with the most limited means.

HEINRICH HEINE

If we throw mother nature out the window, she comes back in the door with a pitchfork.

MASANOBU FUKUOKA

the thing
        perhaps
    is to eat flowers
and not
        to be

    afraid

e e cummings

The garden suggests

there might be a place where

we can meet nature halfway.

MICHAEL POLLAN

bulb: potential flower
buried in autumn,
never to be seen again.

HENRY BEARD

You
can
bury
a lot of
troubles
digging
in the
dirt.

AUTHOR UNKNOWN

Gardening is the only unquestionably useful job.

GEORGE BERNARD SHAW

Earth laughs in flowers.

RALPH WALDO EMERSON

We learn from our gardens
to deal with the most
urgent question of the time:
How much is enough?

WENDELL BERRY

My green thumb came only as a result
of the mistakes I made while learning to
see things from the plant's point of view.

H. FRED ALE

I think every garden should have plenty of places to sit.

DOUG OSTER

Ever
eat a pine tree?
Many parts are
edible...Yummy.
Do I detect a hint
of blue spruce?

EUELL GIBBONS

Eating what stands on one leg
(mushrooms and plant foods),

is better than eating what
stands on two legs
(fowl),

which is better than eating
what stands on four legs
(cows, pigs, and other animals).

CHINESE PROVERB

It is one thing to live in New York City
and know the farmer who sells you milk
or meat or whatever. It is quite another to
live in New York City and be the farmer.

MANNY HOWARD

More than anything
I must have flowers,
always, always.

CLAUDE MONET

Still, in a way, nobody sees a flower; really.

It is so small. We haven't the time and to see takes time,

like to have friends takes time.

GEORGIA O'KEEFE

The family that gardens together, stays together.

ANONYMOUS

'EVEN IF SOMETHING IS LEFT UNDONE,

'EVERYONE MUST TAKE TIME TO SIT STILL

AND WATCH THE LEAVES TURN.

ELIZABETH LAWRENCE

If dandelions were
hard to grow,
they would be
most welcome
on any lawn.

ANDREW MASON

If I had my life
to live over,
I would start barefoot
earlier in the spring
and stay that way
later in the fall.

NADINE STAIR

VIOLETS SMELL LIKE BURNT SUGAR CUBES
THAT HAVE BEEN DIPPED IN LEMON AND VELVET.

DIANE ACKERMAN

*What will I do
when I can no longer dig?*

KNUTE HAMSON

Do the best that you can
in the place where you are,
and be kind.

SCOTT NEARING

All good work is done the way
ants do things: Little by little.

LAFCADIO HEARN

People from a planet without flowers

would think we must be mad with joy the whole time

to have such things about us.

IRIS MURDOCH

No occupation is so delightful to me
as the culture of the earth,
and no culture comparable
to that of the garden.

THOMAS JEFFERSON

Flowers leave
some of their fragrance
in the hand
that bestows them.

CHINESE PROVERB

One of the most
meaningful gifts we
receive from the food
we grow ourselves
is the gift of story.

LORRAINE JOHNSON

IN GARDENS,
BEAUTY IS A BY-PRODUCT.
THE MAIN BUSINESS IS
SEX AND DEATH.

SAM LLEWELYN

For myself
I hold no preferences among flowers,
so long as they are
wild, free, spontaneous.

EDWARD ABBEY

Forget not

that the earth

delights to feel

your bare feet.

KAHLIL GIBRAN

Teach the children that the soil
is the plant's dinner.

SHARON LOVEJOY

Lovely! See the cloud appear!

Lovely! See the rain, the rain draw near!

Who spoke?

It was the little corn ear

high on the tip of the stalk.

TRADITIONAL ZUNI SONG

LEAVES ARE THE VERBS THAT CONJUGATE THE SEASONS.

GRETEL EHRLICH

If you can paint one leaf you can paint the whole world.

JOHN RUSKIN

I think it pisses God off
if you walk by
the color purple
in a field somewhere
and don't notice it.

ALICE WALKER

Weeds are flowers too, once you get to know them.

A. A. MILNE

You can't be *suspicious* of *a tree,*
or accuse *a bird* or *a squirrel* of *subversion*
or *challenge* the ideology of *a violet.*

HAL BORLAND

THIS GRAND SHOW IS ETERNAL.
IT IS ALWAYS SUNRISE SOMEWHERE.

JOHN MUIR

blessed are the bees
for they make earth
fruitful and green.

MARY DE LA VALETTE

How we spend
our days is,
of course, how we
spend our lives.

ANNIE DILLARD

Despite the gardener's best intentions, Nature will improvise.

MICHAEL GAROFALO

TO BE THE AGENT
            WHOSE TOUCH CHANGES NATURE
FROM A WILD FORCE
            TO A WORK OF ART
                        IS INSPIRATION
            OF THE HIGHEST ORDER.

ROBERT "BOB" RODALE

I love spring anywhere,
but if I could choose
I would always greet it
in a garden.

RUTH STOUT

NOT ONLY WAS THE CREATOR OF LIFE

BRILLIANT BEYOND BELIEF IN MAKING

AN INTRICATELY INTERWOVEN SYSTEM,

BUT ALSO IN WEAVING ASTOUNDING,

BREATH-TAKING, MAGICAL BEAUTY

INTO THE VERY ABILITY OF LIFE TO THRIVE.

JULIA BUTTERFLY HILL

Every part of this earth is sacred to my people.
Every shining pine needle...
Will you teach your children what we have
taught our children, that the earth is our mother?
What befalls the earth befalls the sons of the earth.
The earth does not belong to man.
Man belongs to the earth.

CHIEF SEATTLE

It is the simple things
of life that make living worthwhile,
the sweet fundamental things
such as love and duty, work and rest
and living close to nature.

LAURA INGALLS WILDER

An addiction to gardening is not all bad
when you consider all the other choices in life.

CORA LEE BELL

We gardeners are dreamers

are we not?

That's what we do,

dream about the future,

and grow until we get there.

JESSICA WALLISER

Don't wear perfume in the garden —
unless you want to be pollinated by bees.

ANNE RAVER

We express our gratitude to all the people

whose inspired words appear on these pages.

We thank them for their love of gardening and beauty and nature.

May we all be inspired gardeners, each in our own way.

Other books you might enjoy from St. Lynn's Press:

A Gardener's Notebook: life with my garden
Doug Oster and Jessica Walliser
ISBN: 978-0981961576; $14.95

Grow Organic: over 250 tips and ideas for growing flowers, veggies, lawns and more
Doug Oster and Jessica Walliser
ISBN: 978-0976763161; $18.95

Tomatoes Garlic Basil: the simple pleasures of growing and cooking your garden's most versatile veggies
Doug Oster
ISBN: 978-0981961514; $18.95

Good Bug Bad Bug: who's who, what they do, and how to manage them organically (all you need to know about the insects in your garden)
Jessica Walliser
ISBN: 978-0981961590; $17.95

Good Weed Bad Weed: who's who, what to do, and why some deserve a second chance (all you need to know about the weeds in your yard)
Nancy Gift
ISBN: 978-0981961569; $17.95

Good Mushroom Bad Mushroom: who's edible, who's toxic, and how to tell the difference (all you need to know about finding and preparing edible wild mushrooms)
John Plischke III
ISBN: 78-0981961583; $17.95

Eat Your Roses...pansies, lavender, and 49 other delicious edible flowers
Denise Schreiber
ISBN: 978-0981961552; $17.95

Find out more about these and other St. Lynn's books and authors online at www.stlynnspress.com